Finding the Fountain of Youth

University Press of Florida

Florida A&M University, Tallahassee
Florida Atlantic University, Boca Raton
Florida Gulf Coast University, Ft. Myers
Florida International University, Miami
Florida State University, Tallahassee

New College of Florida, Sarasota
University of Central Florida, Orlando
University of Florida, Gainesville
University of North Florida, Jacksonville
University of South Florida, Tampa
University of West Florida, Pensacola

Finding the Fountain of Youth

Ponce de León and Florida's Magical Waters

Rick Kilby

University Press of Florida
Gainesville · Tallahassee · Tampa · Boca Raton
Pensacola · Orlando · Miami · Jacksonville · Ft. Myers · Sarasota

A Florida Quincentennial Book

Copyright 2013 by Rick Kilby
Printed in Korea on acid-free paper

18 17 16 15 14 13   6 5 4 3 2 1

Library of Congress Cataloging-in-Publication Data
Kilby, Rick.
Finding the fountain of youth : Ponce de León and
Florida's magical waters / Rick Kilby.
p. cm.
Includes bibliographical references.
ISBN 978-0-8130-4487-3 (alk. paper)
1. Fountain of youth (Legendary place)—Pictorial works. 2. Ponce de
León, Juan, 1460?–1521—Pictorial works. 3. Florida—Discovery and
exploration—Pictorial works. 4. Florida—History. 5. Florida—Description
and travel. I. Title.
GR941.F68K55 2013
398.209759—dc23   2012046697

University Press of Florida
15 Northwest 15th Street
Gainesville, FL 32611-2079
http://www.upf.com

The author at the Fountain of Youth attraction in St. Augustine in the 1960s.

To my parents, who raised me
in the Land of Flowers

TELF. { M-5031
A-0004
LA FLORIDA
Obispo & Monserrate Sts.
HABANA - CUBA
BAR RESTAURANT
THE CRADLE OF THE DAIQUIRI COCKTAIL
PONCE DE LEON DISCOVERING IN THE "LA FLORIDA BAR"
THE FOUNTAIN OF ETERNAL YOUTH

✦ Contents ✦

Introduction: How I Found the Fountain of Youth 1

1. Ponce de León and the Myth of the Fountain of Youth 9

2. Magic in the Waters: The Fantasy of Florida Beckons Newcomers 29

3. Marketing the Myth: Inventing an American Eden 59

4. Swimming Holes to Sinkholes: Turning Crystal Waters into Liquid Gold 87

Acknowledgments 125

Bibliography 127

Image Credits 131

Above: Ponce de León was once featured widely in brochures for Florida attractions; this image is from the Miami Wax Museum.

Right: De Leon Springs in Central Florida continues to be a popular state park.

How I Found the Fountain of Youth

In 1513, Juan Ponce de León stepped onto a beach in Florida, and five hundred years later, we're still walking in his footsteps. The Spanish explorer's mythical connection with a Fountain of Youth has had an enduring effect on the development of the Sunshine State.

Historians now tell us that Ponce's fabled search for magical, rejuvenating waters is fiction, a story that began years after his death in 1521. Like other European explorers, Ponce sought new territories in search of "wealth, titles, power, and prestige," as historian J. Michael Francis has written. "There is no historical evidence to suggest that Ponce was even aware of the fabled spring, let alone that he risked life and fortune on a quest to locate it."

But as Francis also notes, the tale of Ponce's quest for a Fountain of Youth has become so deeply interwoven in the fabric of Florida's identity that it has become a part of our past, transcending myth to attain its own kind of reality. I've found that buying into the myth has shaped Floridians' choices and even our identity. In some cases, that has been harmful to our state.

REVELATION AT THE "TOURIST TRAP"

My own personal journey to the Fountain of Youth began a few years ago at Thanksgiving, when my family gathered for the holiday weekend in St. Augustine. My wife and I arrived early to take in some of the sights, and our first stop was the vintage Fountain of Youth attraction, which was near our hotel. It was both kitschy and historic, and I loved it. Mannequins in period garb surrounded a small "spring" near rocks laid in the shape of a cross—said to mark the year of Ponce's arrival. A planetarium featured a presentation demonstrating how Spanish explorers navigated across the sea using only stars. Displays portrayed recent archaeological finds at the site. Peacocks wandered the lush grounds.

That visit to the Fountain of Youth offered a glimpse into a whole new world. It went against years of conditioning: When I was a boy, my parents had carefully steered clear of Florida's roadside attractions, deeming them "tourist traps." While it can't be compared with today's mega–theme parks, I found the Fountain of Youth to be fun, interesting, and beautiful.

> In lyrical song and soulful meditation, the idea of Florida as a place of youth and renewal persists as a powerful metaphor. . . . Ponce de León's quest for the Fountain of Youth incorporates Florida's birth myth, a perfect symbol for a state obsessed with second chances and eternal exuberance.
>
> **Gary Mormino, Land of Sunshine, State of Dreams**

Whitney's Ponce de Leon Spring, St. Augustine, Fla.

Above: One of the earliest hucksters to exploit the Fountain of Youth myth was St. Augustine businessman John Whitney, who in 1870 declared a small spring on his property was the fabled fountain.

Right: A vintage citrus label shows Ponce de León discovering the Fountain of Youth in the juice of an orange.

¡¡Eureka!!

THE FOUNTAIN OF YOUTH

WAS REALLY USÓ'S ORANGE JUICE!

MANUEL USÓ & CíA. VALENCIA

I wondered if other Floridians, jaded by constant marketing to tourists, have missed out on some of the coolest stuff our state has to offer. I made it my mission to see aspects of Florida I had ignored in the past and to write a blog about my adventures, in an effort to raise awareness about the overlooked and underappreciated side of Florida.

ON THE TRAIL OF REAL FLORIDA

My first excursions were to Wakulla Springs in the Panhandle and Weeki Wachee near Brooksville. I also stopped at the Stephen Foster Memorial at White Springs and visited the site of an old health spa on the banks of the Suwannee River. Then, on a trip to De Leon Springs in Volusia County, I noticed the recurring narrative that connects many Florida springs.

The story goes like this. First, the spring is a sacred place to the Native Americans living in the region. Then, colonial settlers homestead nearby, drawn by the cool, pure water. As early tourists start to make their way into the state toward the end of the nineteenth century, steamboats journey to some of these springs, and others become health spas, as entrepreneurs consciously exploit the Fountain of Youth myth when northerners come to "take the waters." Many more visitors arrive in the state after Henry Plant and Henry Flagler develop their railroad empires.

With the arrival of the twentieth century, tourists start to arrive by car, roadside attractions pop up, and Florida's springs transition from spas with healing waters to tourist attractions with fanciful features including water-skiing elephants and performing mermaids. Eventually, interstate highways bypass many of the roadside attractions at these beloved springs, and most morph into state parks. Now, in the twenty-first century, many of our

Top right: An archival brochure links good health to oranges and grapefruit, deemed the "Health Fruits of Florida."

Below right: Attracted to the healthy lifestyle portrayed by Florida's promoters, seniors came to the state in droves in the years after World War II.

An advertisement features a colorful conquistador on a Segway in St. Augustine, dubbed the nation's oldest city.

state's "fountains of youths" are at risk, as development pressures threaten the springs and the peninsula's underground aquifer.

I found the same or similar narratives at springs around the state. In addition to two springs named after Ponce de León, many natural springs claimed to be the original Fountain of Youth, from the Panhandle's Wakulla Springs to Warm Mineral Springs near Venice. Even several man-made springs, most notably wells drilled in St. Petersburg, claimed to be the true Fountain of Youth.

I also became aware that, although Floridians once celebrated Ponce de León by putting his name on everything from street signs to motels, he fell out of favor at some point. As I continued my quest, I understood more about that part of the story—how historians now understand the importance of a multicultural perspective, including the perspective of the Native Americans who "discovered" Florida long before Ponce.

KEEPING THE MYTH ALIVE

And so I found myself drawn to the story of Ponce and his fabled Fountain of Youth because the story of the mythical, magical waters is in so many ways the story of Florida. I started a survey of all things related to the myth, first with my own photography and later by collecting photos, postcards, brochures—whatever I could find that was related to the Fountain of Youth.

I've collected my visual treasures into this book, to tell the story of my state and its magical waters through the artifacts and images of popular culture. I believe that many of the wonderful, unique places in the Sunshine State are at risk, and that by creating more understanding and awareness of how special they are, we may be able to preserve them for future generations. The Fountain of Youth of legend was a gateway to eternity. And while it is impossible to stop the forces of nature in real life, perhaps we can maintain our one-of-a-kind places for our descendants to enjoy, thus keeping the myth alive.

Left: Ponce de León's influence remains visible in numerous cities throughout Florida; many streets continue to bear his name.

Below: St. Augustine's recently restored Bridge of Lions is guarded by this fierce-looking lion with "P de L 1513" inscribed at the base, honoring the Spanish explorer.

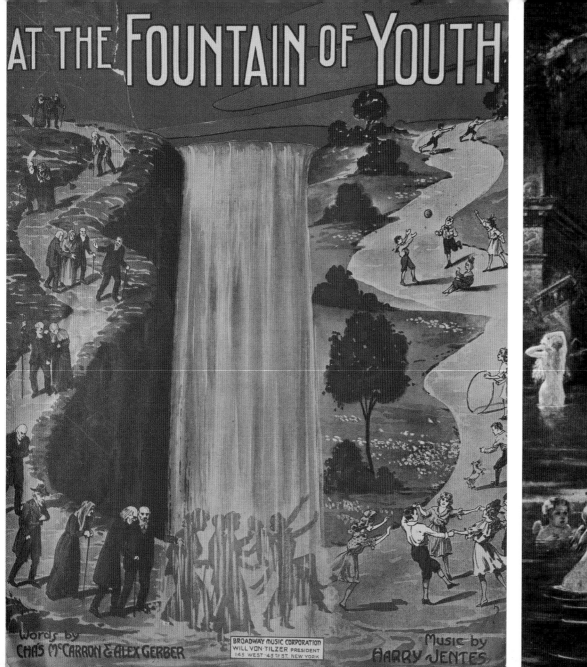

THE ENDLESS SEARCH.

PONCE DE LEON. — They laugh at me, but they still keep it up!

→ 1 ←

Ponce de León and the Myth of the Fountain of Youth

Separating Fact from Fiction
in Ponce's Land of Flowers

Every kid growing up in Florida learns that the Spanish explorer Ponce de León led the first bunch of Europeans to land on the peninsula, on April 2, 1513. And for decades, they were also taught that Ponce was on a special quest. Textbooks such as *La Florida: Its Land and People* (1957) explained that he "had heard the stories told by natives of a miraculous fountain . . . where waters would restore one to youth again." Even the venerable *WPA Guide to Florida* (1939), compiled by the Federal Writers' Project, included the tale that Ponce sought a "magic fountain that restored youth."

Perhaps the story had such staying power because Florida's waters have always been tremendously important to its people. As Florida author Bill Belleville has written, "Water has shaped culture in Florida from the very first moment humans stepped foot on this ancient sea-bottom terrace" 12,000 years ago, at the end of the Ice Age. Scholars now tell us that when Ponce arrived, about 350,000 Native Americans lived in what would become Florida.

The largest group, the Timucua, lived on the northern half of the peninsula and had been here for thousands of years before Europeans arrived. The Timucua revered the waters of Florida—and all of nature—as sacred. Water shaped the culture of these people, as it shapes our culture today. But in the quest that led Ponce to Florida, sacred water was the last thing he was seeking.

THE REAL PONCE

Here's what most historians now think are the facts about the Spaniard who named Florida.

Born to a noble family in the Castilla region of Spain in 1474, Juan Ponce de León was a veteran of Spain's wars with the Moors by the time he was a teenager and, in 1493, he sailed with Christopher Columbus on Columbus's second voyage to the New World. Ponce was eventually rewarded with the governorship of the island of Hispaniola, and founded the first European colony on the island of Puerto Rico, where he was also named governor in 1509.

Juan Ponce is best remembered for something he did not find—a magic fountain, the pursuit of which was not even his idea—while all but forgotten are his important discoveries.

Robert H. Fuson, Juan Ponce de León and the Spanish Discovery of Puerto Rico and Florida

Left: A 1970 advertisement for MONY insurance shows the pervasiveness of the myth.

But after a court in Spain ruled that Christopher Columbus's son Diego had a right to lands discovered by his father, the younger Columbus assumed leadership of Puerto Rico. Ponce received a royal charter to explore the islands north of Puerto Rico, including Bimini—possibly the location of a rejuvenating fountain, according to native legend. Ponce's detailed charter gave him dominion over this island but made no mention of such a fountain. On March 3, 1513, he sailed north by northwest from Puerto Rico with three ships.

Above: "How the Natives Collect Gold in the Streams," an engraving by Theodor de Bry, based on artwork by Jacques Le Moyne de Morgues. Le Moyne's images of Timucuan Indians constitute the best visual record of Native Americans in Florida at the time of European exploration, although it is unknown how accurate they actually are.

Facing page: A vintage engraving shows Ponce de León, center, holding a goblet filled from the famed Fountain of Youth. Based on archetypes and myths from other cultures, the legend has persisted into the twenty-first century.

Ponce de Leon.

The explorers made landfall March 8 on what may have been Grand Turk and on April 2 came upon what they thought was another island. "They called it *La Florida*," according to the best-known account of the journey, written by court historian Antonio de Herrera, "because it had a very beautiful view of many and cool woodlands, and it was level and uniform; and because, moreover, they discovered it in the time of the Feast of Flowers [Pascua Florida]."

So where did Ponce come ashore? We may never know with certainty, but the St. Augustine area, New Smyrna Beach, and Melbourne Beach are among the top contenders. His expedition stayed for several days and, after departing about April 8 and sailing south along the coast, made its second great discovery: the Florida Current, or the Gulf Stream. Knowledge of the powerful current would prove useful for future return trips to Europe. Ironically, unlike the mythical Fountain of Youth, it was a significant find for which Ponce de León is not popularly remembered.

SEARCH FOR THE FOUNTAIN OF YOUTH.

Apparently Ponce did not encounter any Native Americans on his initial landing, but at his next couple of landfalls along Florida's east coast, he and his men had violent encounters with Indians. (Some historians think earlier, unrecorded groups of European slave hunters may have landed before Ponce, making the natives wary of intruders, but the sight of Ponce's sailing ship and his men would have been terrifying in any case.) Ponce continued along the coast of south Florida, reaching the upper Florida Keys on May 13, and sailed to Key West before heading up the west coast of the peninsula, where he again fought with Native Americans.

After nine days on the west coast of Florida, the expedition headed south and stopped at the Dry Tortugas before returning to Puerto Rico via Cuba. One of Ponce's three ships sailed to the Bahamas to search for Bimini and returned to Puerto Rico four months later.

In 1521, Ponce again sailed to La Florida in an attempt to establish a colony there. Landing at San Carlos Bay on the southwest coast, the expedition encountered Calusa Indians who attacked them, wounding Ponce with an arrow in the thigh. After retreating to Cuba, he died from an infection caused by the wound.

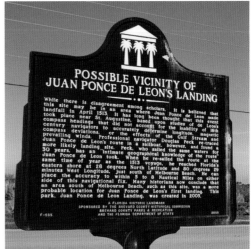

While in search of the Fountain of Youth, Juan Ponce de Leon and his companions visited Wakulla Springs both in 1513 and 1521. On his second visit Ponce de Leon was wounded by an arrow in an attack by Indians. He was taken to Cuba, where he died shortly after from the effects of this wound. The blood-stained arrow with which he was supposedly shot is in the permanent collection at the Lodge. The adjacent area is rich in historical lore and ruins of old Spanish and English forts may still be seen on the Wakulla River.

Wakulla Springs — 20 Miles South of Tallahassee, Fla. 243

Above: Juan Ponce de León Landing Park in Brevard County pays tribute to the fact that some historians think Ponce first made landfall in La Florida near Melbourne Beach.

Left: A plaque below this statue of the Spanish explorer at the Fountain of Youth Archaeological Park in St. Augustine reads: "He named this land, first seen here, 'La Florida.'"

Facing page: Historical markers at Punta Gorda (*left*) and Juan Ponce de León Landing in Brevard County (*right*) honor the explorer and his landing in Florida; a postcard from Wakulla Springs near Tallahassee claims that Ponce was fatally wounded while visiting the Panhandle.

THE MYTH THAT WON'T DIE

In his book *Juan Ponce de León and the Spanish Discovery of Puerto Rico and Florida*, historian Robert Fuson suggests that Ponce's search for Bimini might indeed have been inspired by its purported magical fountain, a legend that originated with the Taíno Indians native to the Bahamas.

Ponce may have had it in the back of his mind, on a list of resources to investigate "in the lands he was about to visit." But, as Fuson also notes, "There is no evidence that Juan Ponce made any serious effort to locate the Fountain of Youth—he certainly did not make any overland marches to Florida's numerous Artesian springs." Ponce's real goals, historians say, were to claim land for Spain that might yield gold and slaves to build the king's empire.

Yet, Ponce remains forever linked to the myth of the Fountain of Youth. It's an association that began a long time ago, decades after Ponce's death, in the works of Antonio de Herrera—a chronicler of Spanish exploration who apparently was relying on a story by another chronicler, the Italian-born Peter Martyr d'Anghiera. That's how the eminent Florida historian Michael Gannon explains the source of the whole mess.

But it's no wonder that the Fountain of Youth won't let Ponce go. It's a powerful myth, with deep roots in our psyches. Why Europeans were susceptible to such far-fetched fables of youth-inducing fountains has a long and varied history indeed.

Fueling the Myth of the Fountain of Youth

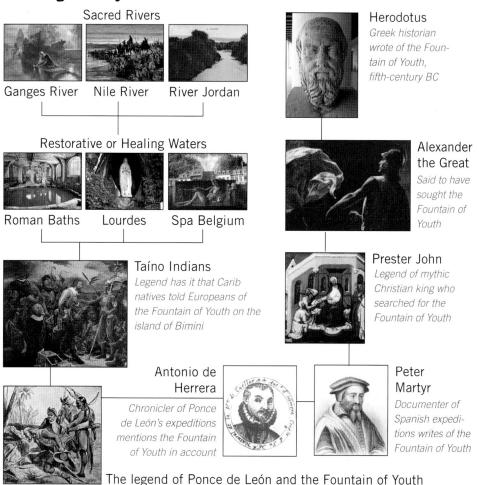

Sacred Rivers

Ganges River   Nile River   River Jordan

Restorative or Healing Waters

Roman Baths   Lourdes   Spa Belgium

Taíno Indians
Legend has it that Carib natives told Europeans of the Fountain of Youth on the island of Bimini

Antonio de Herrera
Chronicler of Ponce de León's expeditions mentions the Fountain of Youth in account

Herodotus
Greek historian wrote of the Fountain of Youth, fifth-century BC

Alexander the Great
Said to have sought the Fountain of Youth

Prester John
Legend of mythic Christian king who searched for the Fountain of Youth

Peter Martyr
Documenter of Spanish expeditions writes of the Fountain of Youth

The legend of Ponce de León and the Fountain of Youth

Fountain Everlasting, time without end! Fountain Everlasting, time without end! Soaring flame of the spirit transfiguring Death! All is within! All things dissolve, flow on eternally! O aspiring fire of life, sweep the dark soul of man! Let us burn in thy unity!

Eugene O'Neill, The Fountain

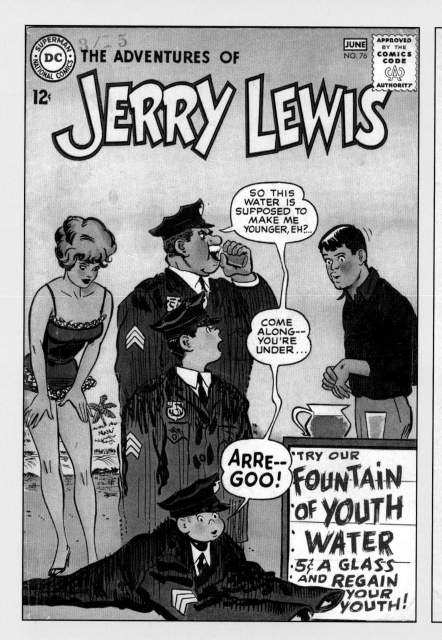

Tootsie Roll makes HISTORY!

History says, Ponce de Leon from Spain
For the Fountain of Youth searched in vain
But really his goal
Was the great **Tootsie Roll**
Which brought pleasure again and again.

AMERICA'S FAVORITE CANDY!

Tootsie Roll

CAP'N CRUNCH AND THE FOUNTAIN OF YOUTH

YOU SHOULD JOIN US FOR
THE WATER SPORTS

I FOUND THE FOUNTAIN
OF YOUTH AGAIN

DISCOVERED 1513 BY PONCE DE LEON

Ponce de León: From Discovery to Disappearance

The county in which Florida's capital is located is named Leon after Ponce de León. A town in the Panhandle, in Holmes County, also bears the explorer's name. Multistory Ponce de León hotels once welcomed guests in Miami and St. Petersburg, as did Ponce de León motels in Florida cities including Daytona Beach and Tallahassee. The 1950s Ponce de León shopping center still stands in St. Augustine, as does the newer Ponce de León Mall. And most older cities in the state have a Ponce de León street, avenue, circle, or boulevard.

Yet at some point in the twentieth century, Floridians began to turn their backs on the first European to set foot in their state, and Ponce fell into disfavor. As a clearer picture of Florida's history emerged, we abandoned the almost comical image of a Spaniard who searched in vain for the mythical antidote to aging. We learned much more about Florida's native peoples, and our perspective shifted. Ponce de León was no longer seen as a buffoon or a hero, but one of the first in the line of Europeans who contributed to the eventual demise of the thousands of years of Native American culture.

The more famous Columbus, with whom Ponce sailed as a young man, had a more dramatic fall from grace. In the early 1990s, anthropologist William F. Keegan noted that the man long hailed as a great hero had come to be "reviled as a symbol of European expansionism, the forbearer of institutionalized racism and genocide who bears ultimate responsibility for everything from the destruction of rainforests to the depletion of the ozone layer." To get at the real Columbus, Keegan noted, it was important to go beyond the facades of both the "discovery" and the "destroyer."

Although Ponce isn't generally associated with the heinous acts committed by some other conquistadors, all European explorers of the "Age of Discovery" lost the idealized, rosy glow that once surrounded them in textbooks and popular histories. This paradigm shift cast Florida's Ponce "brand" in a new light. The man who named Florida once appeared on ads for everything from spas to citrus, but today "Ponceabilia"—relics from the era when the explorer's image was used to promote Florida—can seem dated if not outright bizarre.

Above: Ads for the Ponce de León Hotel in Miami claimed that "its restful dignity forms a perfect setting for the Winter life of Miami . . . All rooms modern in every respect . . . Cuisine and Service unexcelled."

Facing page, top left: Signage for the Ponce de León Mall in St. Augustine. *Bottom left*: Current image of Hotel Ponce de León in St. Petersburg. *Right*: Detail of flagpole in St. Augustine.

Evidence of the sometimes kitschy Ponce "brand" still survives in Florida, however, if one looks closely enough. In fact, the image of the legendary conquistador can still be found extensively throughout St. Augustine. There is also a recently erected statue of Ponce in Punta Gorda, and the long-deceased explorer apparently has endorsed the spa at Warm Mineral Springs near Venice.

Ponce de León has inspired a statue in Punta Gorda (*left*) and advertising for Warm Mineral Springs in North Port (*above*).

Facing page: The Hotel Ponce de León in St. Petersburg shines in a 1950s postcard.

Ponce de Leon Motel, Tallahassee, Florida

INTERIOR OF SPRING,
WHITE SPRINGS FLA.

12401

⇥2⇤

Magic in the Waters:
The Fantasy of Florida Beckons Newcomers

Florida Fast Forward: From Sacred Waters to Miracle Cures

If you visit the many places in Florida that have claimed ties to the Fountain of Youth, you might get the impression that Ponce de León stumbled across the peninsula, drinking from every spring he could find in search of the elusive elixir. Contemporary historians tend to agree that this perception is based on legend, not fact. But the image of Florida as the land of life-giving waters has persisted, even as the rest of the fable has been debunked. That image has been consciously exploited to entice more and more visitors to the Land of Flowers, where the geography features the largest concentration of springs in the world (more than seven hundred).

Florida's springs were revered by the peninsula's inhabitants for thousands of years before Ponce stepped foot on its sandy shores. When he arrived, about 350,000 native people made Florida their home, historian Michael Gannon tells us. They included about 50,000 Apalachee around present-day Tallahassee, 150,000 Timucua in the northern half of the peninsula, and 150,000 others in the Panhandle and central and southern Florida. They had long hunted, farmed, and fished throughout what is now Florida, and they considered many of its springs to be sacred sites.

The Seminoles, who would migrate south into Florida in the 1700s, also revered Florida's waters. Their eloquent war leader Coacoochee once spoke about a dream in which his dead twin sister "visited him from the land of souls, offering him a cup of pure water from the spring of the Great Spirit," Bill Belleville writes. "And if I should drink of it," Coacoochee said, "I should return and live with her forever."

"Archaeological evidence indicates that people have been attracted to Florida's springs for thousands of years," according to the state's Department of Environmental Protection website. "The springs made the perfect home for Native Floridians who used them as a source of water and food, while the clay taken from the spring's bottom was ideal for making arrowheads, spear heads, and knives."

Sadly, by the late 1700s, those native Floridians were no more. As Jerald Milanich has written, the European presence that began with Ponce "brought diseases and slaving

> The brave warrior Cooacoochee hid out with a band of 200 in the wild swamps of the Wekiva River ... [he] reported the spirit of his twin sister once visited him from the land of souls, offering him a cup of pure water from the spring of the Great Spirit. "And if I should drink of it," said Cooacoochee, "I should return and live with her forever."
>
> **Bill Belleville, Forum magazine**

Florida's frontier, post Ponce

Indigenous people of Florida during the age of European contact: People of the Timucua, Apalachee, Ais, Tekesta, and Calusa revered and used the peninsula's springs.

Spanish explorers Hernando de Soto (1539), Tristán de Luna y Arellano (1559), and Pedro Menéndez de Avilés (1565) land in Florida.

Great Soft-shelled Tortoise.

Florida's largest early European settlements are on its coasts: St. Augustine, Jacksonville, Key West, and Pensacola.

The United States fights three wars against the Seminole Indians between 1817 and 1858. The major conflict, the Second Seminole War (1835–1842), is the most costly Indian war ever waged by the United States.

Naturalist William Bartram explores Florida in 1774.

During the Civil War, Florida plays a critical role in supplying the Confederacy with cattle and salt.

In the 1870s northerners begin visiting Florida.

raids" that "ultimately destroyed Florida's original inhabitants." By the 1800s, three wars with the United States had reduced the Seminoles from a population of about 4,000 to just a few hundred people.

Three hundred years before, in the 1500s, a secession of European explorers from Narváez to de Soto made their way through Florida after Ponce's landing. It took the Europeans some time to become established, even though they put down roots decades before Jamestown or Massachusetts. In 1565, Don Pedro Menéndez de Avilés established the first successful colony at St. Augustine. Although the British and the French would become players in Florida's colonial history, the Spanish were in charge through most of the next two centuries. The Brits briefly took control in 1763, but after the Revolutionary War, Spain regained La Florida, which became a U.S. territory in 1822 and a state in 1845. On the eve of the Civil War, 347 years after Ponce's landing, only about 140,000 people lived in all of Florida, and more than 40 percent of them were enslaved. It was not until after the war's end that a significant number of visitors began to discover Florida's magical waters for themselves.

METAMORA

METAMORA OF PALATKA.

LUCAS' NEW LINE.

THELMA

014233. SILVER SPRINGS ON THE OCKLAWAHA, FLORIDA.

DETROIT PHOTOGRAPHIC CO.

The state was settled from the outside in: Coastal towns were the only real population centers throughout most of the eighteenth and nineteenth centuries. Because of the lack of roads, the main route into the state was by water, and in the nineteenth century, steamboats begin venturing into the interior of the peninsula via the St. Johns River and its tributaries.

The rest of the nation had begun to learn about the exotic land of Florida through fantastic written accounts. In 1791, the naturalist William Bartram published his famed *Travels*, in which he detailed the flora and fauna of what was then known as East Florida. Bartram's accounts of Florida's springs must have fed the imaginations of readers already familiar with the Fountain of Youth legend. He described one spring as an "enchanting and amazing crystal fountain" and compared Florida's waters to "the blue ether of another world."

Steamboats at Silver Springs landing proved popular subjects for photographers, including George Barker in 1886 (*above*) and William Henry Jackson in 1902 (*facing page*).

After the Civil War, *Uncle Tom's Cabin* author Harriet Beecher Stowe became another early advocate for Florida, through her book *Palmetto Leaves*, a compilation of stories about living in Florida on the St. Johns River near Jacksonville. In a chapter titled "Florida for Invalids," Stowe wrote: "If persons suffer constitutionally from cold; if they are bright and well only in hot weather; if the winter chills and benumbs them, till, in the spring, they are in the condition of a frost-bitten hot-house plant—alive, to be sure, but with every leaf gone—then these persons may be quite sure they will be better for a winter in Florida, and better still if they can take up their abode there."

Florida as a land of eternal health soon became a theme of early Florida promoters, according to historian Tracy J. Revels in her book *Sunshine Paradise: A History of Florida Tourism.* "Promising cures they could not deliver, physicians and boosters conspired with local entrepreneurs to initiate the first wave of Florida tourism," Revels writes. "They began building Florida's reputation as a sunshine paradise, a land of fantasies and dreams."

Right: The Brock House in Enterprise advertised "high land and dry air." The hotel was reported to be one of the largest frame buildings in the nation in the 1850s.

Facing page: Steamboats such as the Osceola opened up the interior of the state for tourists; roads adequate for automobile traffic were not available until the early twentieth century.

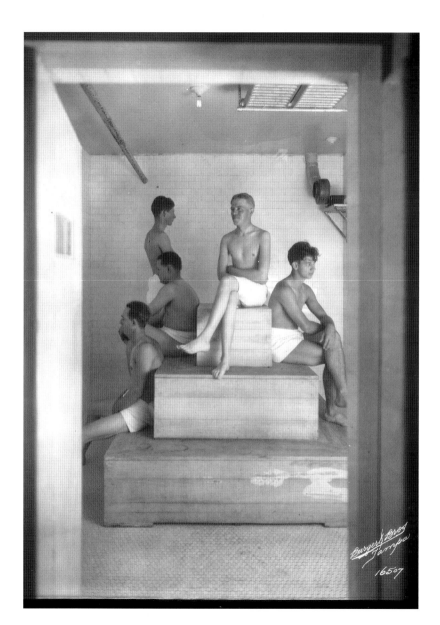

Beginning in the late nineteenth century, the coastal towns of St. Augustine and Key West attracted tourists looking for better health. Inland entrepreneurs developed health spas around several Florida springs and along the St. Johns River. Spas opened at White Springs and Suwannee Springs along the Suwannee River, according to Revels, and on other rivers: Orange Springs on the Ocklawaha, Green Cove Springs on the St. Johns, Worthington Springs on the Santa Fe, Newport Springs on the St. Marks. Panacea Mineral Springs touted its healing powers in the Panhandle, and Hampton Springs counted even Theodore Roosevelt a visitor to its sulfur-laced waters near Perry. The spa at Safety Harbor, originally known as Espiritu Santo Springs, opened in the 1890s and is still operating today.

Left: The Burgert Brothers photographers of Tampa captured an image of towel-clad spa-goers at Safety Harbor Spa, originally known as Espiritu Santo Springs. Discovered by Spanish explorer Hernando De Soto, these springs were advertised as the famed Fountain of Youth.

Facing page: Gilded Age visitors gather in the 1880s around a pool at Green Cove Springs, where the sulfur-laced waters began attracting visitors in the 1850s.

At these spas, the miraculous waters of Florida were said to cure everything from consumption and jaundice to rheumatism and syphilis. One ad for Florida even claimed the state's climate could help "stimulate the faculty of reproduction." While many of these springs continue to flow today, the facilities that surrounded them are a distant memory; most of the large wooden hotels of the nineteenth century that were devoted to restorative health exist only in photographs.

Postcards advertise Green Cove Springs (*right*) and Hampton Springs in Taylor County (*facing page*). *Far right*: Staff members await visitors at the Clarendon Hotel in Green Cove Springs.

Guaranteed for Rheumatism, Indigestion, Dyspepsia, Stomach, Kidney, Bladder Troubles, Gastritis and Skin Diseases.

HAMPTON SPRING WATER
Hotel Hampton
The National Health Resort

HAMPTON SPRINGS
TAYLOR COUNTY
FLORIDA

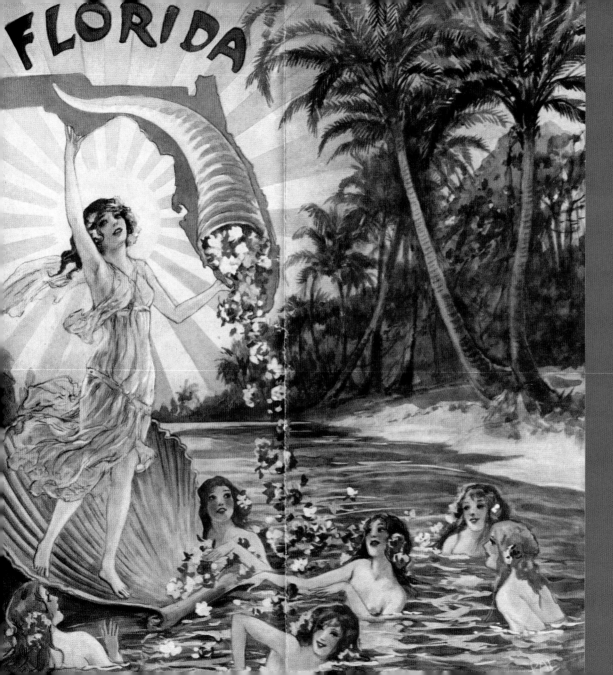

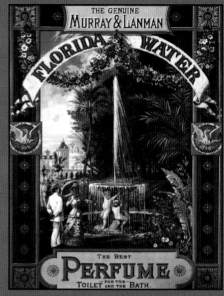

. . . there is a legend which tells of flowers that grow in Paradise eternally in bloom, the perfume of which, when once inhaled insures perpetual happiness, filling the soul with such delight as human tongue can not describe . . .

Murray & Lanman Florida Water advertisement

Victorian-era advertising for Murray & Lanman's Florida Water perfume took advantage of the health-giving reputation of Florida's waters, and featured beautiful women and elaborate fountains.

Right: The Orange City Mineral Spring Co. in Volusia County marketed "an ideal table water."

Facing page (*far left*): An advertisement for Florida shows a Venus-like figure spilling flowers into pristine waters from a cornucopia shaped like the state.

FLORIDA
EAST COAST
RAILWAY AND HOTELS

NASSAU AND CUBA

WHERE WINTER TIME IS JUNE TIME

East Coast of FLORIDA

GENERAL INFORMATION

Left: Promotional brochures for Flagler's East Coast Railway. Ads for the railway such as the one on the facing page proclaimed that the "magic spell of the Gulf Stream" would offer visitors summer magic in winter and the chance to find the "fountain of youth or the fountain of health." The Gulf Stream was discovered by none other than Ponce de León.

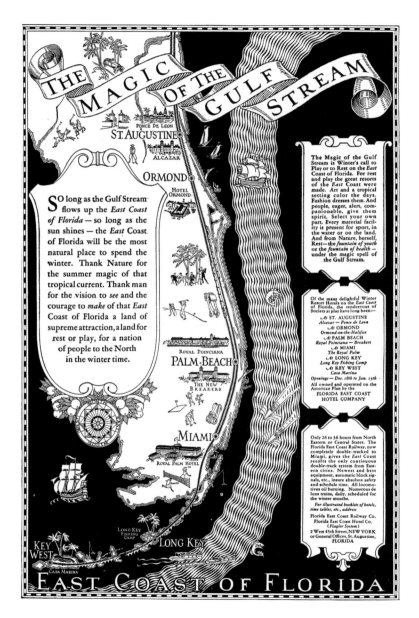

Flagler Builds a New Florida

After the Civil War and Reconstruction, most of Florida was still undeveloped or agrarian. Beginning in the 1870s, steamship lines began bringing tourists into the state's interior via the St. Johns and its scenic tributaries, but railroads proved to be the major engine for the state's modern tourist industry. In the mid 1890s, the state began giving away land to encourage the development of railroads. Soon two railroad magnates, Henry Flagler and Henry Plant, opened up entirely new portions of the state to a public hungry for escape into a land of endless sunshine and abundant health.

Foremost of these entrepreneurs was Flagler, who had made his fortune as John D. Rockefeller's partner in Standard Oil. Like so many other visitors to Florida in the late 1800s, Flagler first came to Florida seeking better health—in his case, for his ailing wife, Mary, who was very ill when they arrived in the winter of 1878. Her health continued to decline, however, and she died in 1881. Two years later, Flagler married her nurse, Ida Alice, and returned to Florida on his honeymoon, staying in St. Augustine.

Flagler saw great potential for the town's development as a resort for the nation's growing elite—one that offered an attractive alternative to Europe's fashionable vacation sites. He used St. Augustine's Spanish heritage as a foundation for creating fantastic buildings based on the architectural style of buildings in the Mediterranean. And in order to make the town more accessible, he got into the business of railroads. He started by purchasing an existing thirty-six-mile railroad in 1888 and kept heading south along Florida's coast until he eventually terminated his railway with a historic extension to Key West in 1912.

Along the way, Flagler created entire towns around resorts such as his Royal Poinciana in Palm Beach and Royal Palm in Miami. To fill his trains and resorts, both Flagler and his rival hotelier, Plant, built upon Florida's reputation for rejuvenation and created a narrative depicting the state as an Eden for tourists weary of northern winters. "Flagler and Plant did much to create the now-familiar image of Florida as a comfortable, pleasurable, even Utopian destination," Susan R. Braden writes in *The Architecture of Leisure*. For his first Florida pleasure palace, Flagler created a hotel of unparalleled grandeur in St. Augustine and named it the Ponce de León. Construction began in 1885 and was completed in 1887.

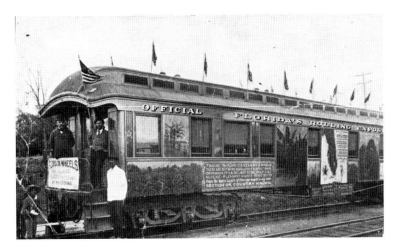

Above: Railroad cars became rolling billboards extolling the virtues of Florida. *Right*: A statue of Henry Flagler stands outside the entrance of St. Augustine's Flagler College, originally the Hotel Ponce de León.

St. Augustine's Ponce de León Celebration was purportedly the inspiration for Flagler to name his first Florida hotel after the Spanish explorer. These photos are from April 6–8, 1927. The graphic is from the 1930 celebration.

Old World Inspiration, New World Grandeur

Inspired by the Moorish architecture of the nearby Villa Zorayda and the Spanish colonial structures throughout the city, Flagler chose to build his magnificent hotel in a Spanish Renaissance style. The "mythic spires" of Flagler's Ponce de León resort reflected "the artist's conception of a Spanish Renaissance palace, not a precise reproduction of one," according to historian Revels, who offers the theory that Flagler's fantastic hotels were a "forerunner of magic kingdoms to come, offering dreams for sale and thematic delights for those who could afford them."

Flagler's Florida East Coast Railway published a promotional booklet, *Ponce de Leon's Fountain of Perpetual Youth*, which offered a fictional "firsthand" account of a couple's stay at the Ponce: "Old travelers that we are, we have never seen anything which approaches it in the artistic quality of its architecture," the husband effused, calling the hotel "a Mecca for the cream of the feathered tourists." Noting that his wife believed that her health was "always greatly benefited by our annual stay," he confessed: "It is my personal belief—which I have not, however, mentioned to her—that she thinks the great fountain in the courtyard of the Hotel Ponce de Leon is the Fountain of Perpetual Youth."

Facing page: Details from the Hotel Ponce de León, which now houses Flagler College. *Following pages*: Postcard views of Flagler's opulent St. Augustine hotel.

Clearly the promotion of the Flagler's Ponce de León, his other Florida hotels, and the luxurious hotels created by Plant on Florida's west coast had a profound effect on the nation's perception of Florida. As author Seth Branson notes, "without the advertising that convinced people to come to Florida via the trains, to stay in the hotels, and to buy the land—all of which were managed by Plant or Flagler organizations—the Florida we know today might not exist."

COURT OF THE PONCE DE LEON.

ST. AUGUSTINE, FLA.

Jan. 31 - 06

A Gusher of Growth in the Twenties

Flagler and Plant opened up entire portions of the state that had been inaccessible before their railroads' arrival. Their empires acquired huge chunks of undeveloped land and helped create a demand for real estate in Florida that peaked during the land boom of the 1920s. Eager investors bought up Florida real estate, hoping to make a fortune and inspired by hype that the state was a place where dreams come true. "Florida captured the spirit of the Jazz Age," authors Nick Wynne and Richard Moorhead write in their book *Paradise for Sale*; Florida was a "tabula rasa that could be whatever a new owner wanted it to be."

Developers drew up plans for new towns and subdivisions carved out of subtropical jungle and in some cases even created entire new islands by dredging waterways. "Hundreds of local developers throughout the state, awed by the money newcomers were willing to spend to buy a slice of these fantasies, quickly set their own architects to drawing plans for new 'old' houses in distinctive subdivisions," Wynne and Moorhead write.

Facing page, top: Real-estate agents in South Florida take potential investors on a tour of future home sites.
Bottom: A 1920s real-estate auction.

Below: Developer D.P. Davis created Davis Island from sand dredged from the bottom of Tampa Bay.

The Boom's Spanish Flavor

Beginning with the resorts and homes of the wealthy, such as Flagler's Ponce de León, the architectural style that best exemplified the fantasy of boom-time Florida was Mediterranean Revival—a style that combines "Moorish, Spanish Colonial, Mission, and Italianate" influences, according to *Tropical Splendor: An Architectural History of Florida*. In the 1920s, the "Spanish boom" style, which spread from expensive homes to simpler family dwellings, "psychologically and economically suited the time and place."

In South Florida, architect Addison Mizner prospered by creating Florida houses that were the polar opposites of the more traditional homes he created for his wealthy clients up north. Buyers of smaller houses sought miniature versions of the same fanciful vision, often featuring inlaid-tile floors, turrets, mini-towers, and balconies, according to Wynne and Moorhead. In her article "Inventing Antiquity: The Art and Craft of Mediterranean Revival Architecture," Beth Dunlop sums up the relevance of this style: "But Florida itself was an invention, a tropical wonderland built on swamp and muck by canny and imaginative entrepreneurs, and it stands to reason that the Mediterranean Revival architecture that would come to symbolize this made-up place would be made-up as well." To this day, the Mediterranean Revival style based on the blend of historic European elements, combined in new, imaginative ways, flourishes throughout Florida.

Above and below: Images by the Burgert Brothers Commercial Photography Studio in Tampa depict some of the newly created Mediterranean Revival structures of the 1920s boom. *Facing page*: Mediterranean Revival architecture from around the state. *Following pages*: Advertisement for the Mediterranean Revival-themed development of Coral Gables in South Florida.

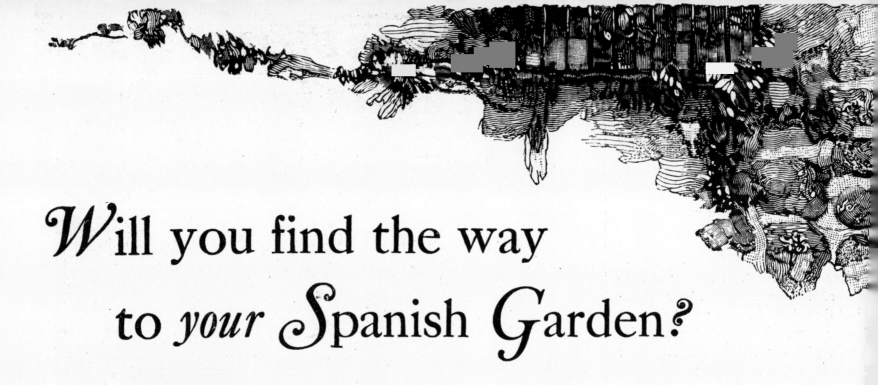

Will you find the way to *your* Spanish Garden?

CREAM STUCCO. Scarlet hibiscus. Black iron grilles. High above, the whispering fronds of a coconut palm. A great red jar in the corner. A table set for luncheon on the cool, tiled floor. A brilliant splotch of sun on the wall. *Your* Spanish garden? Why not? . . . You can have a home in Coral Gables in the picturesque manner of old Seville, decorated in perfect taste, with a garden that takes you back to the days of Spanish domain. It will cost you no more than an ordinary home on a dingy city street—*and its value must increase as the city plan matures, and as the new developments approach completion.*

CORAL GABLES
Miami Riviera
40 Miles of Water Front
GEORGE E. MERRICK

✦ 3 ✦

Marketing the Myth:
Inventing an American Eden

PONCE de LEON *HAD THE RIGHT IDEA!*

Selling the Land
of Perpetual Rejuvenation

In 1925 alone, more than 2.5 million people rushed into Florida "looking for 50 feet of paradise," in the words of historian Michael Gannon. But the 1920s land boom began to collapse after the great Miami hurricane of 1926, followed by the devastating Okeechobee storm of 1928, and the Great Depression came early to Florida. It wasn't until World War II that a whole new wave of visitors got a look at the Land of Flowers, when the state served as the training ground for more than 2 million military personnel. Many of the grand hotels from the days of Flagler and Plant and the 1920s boom were pressed into service as barracks and hospitals during the war, including the grand Ponce de León in St. Augustine and the Biltmore in Coral Gables.

This was the beginning of the golden age of Florida tourism, as "uniformed hordes of military guests" descended on existing attractions, and enterprising entrepreneurs including Cypress Gardens' Dick Pope developed and marketed parks to capitalize on the captive military audience, as historian Tracy Revels has noted. After the war, many GIs returned to Florida with their families, some on vacation, some to stay as permanent residents.

State tourism officials recognized the value of drawing visitors to Florida and began aggressively promoting the state as a tropical paradise where fantasies come to life. "There is a fountain of Youth in Florida, but it doesn't bubble from the ground as P. De Leon thought," effused a midcentury advertisement. "It's in the very air you breathe here where the land is washed by pure sea breezes containing 20 percent more oxygen than air in landlocked regions."

The golden age of Florida tourism in the twentieth century was the era of the roadside attraction where "fantasies could be glimpsed for the price of a ticket," as Revels writes. And many of the state's most enduring tourist attractions revolved around the enduring myth of the Fountain of Youth—none more so than the St. Augustine establishment that identifies itself as the actual spot Ponce de León was seeking.

Florida was advertised as the answer to hard luck, misfortune, even death.

John Rothchild, Up for Grabs

Here's the bright answer to winter's chills and ills . . . a fast move near the sun . . . a full charge of that fabulous sense of well-being which makes everything you see and do seem extra special!

Advertising copy from the State of Florida

Myth Meets Archaeology:
St. Augustine's Fountain of Youth

There is solid archaeological evidence that the grounds of the Fountain of Youth attraction in St. Augustine were once the location of a Timucuan Indian village led by a chief named Seloy. There is also evidence that the first Spanish settlement of Pedro Menéndez in 1565 was on the site as well; the Indians apparently allowed the Europeans to settle in their community. More controversial, however, is the site's connection to Ponce de León.

According to a booklet produced in 1956 by the attraction's then-owner, Walter Fraser, the current grounds of the park were originally part of three Spanish land grants purchased by H. H. Williams in 1868. Williams discovered a cross made of coquina rock near a spring, the booklet continues—but he buried the cross, and it remained that way until it was uncovered by the property's next owners, Dr. Luella Day McConnell and her husband, Edward.

FOUNTAIN OF YOUTH, ST. AUGUSTINE, FLA.

Top: Humorous postcard illustrating the effects of the fountain. *Bottom*: Postcard showing the well at St. Augustine's Fountain of Youth.

Facing page: Illustration from a vintage brochure and postcard for the attraction.

Dr. McConnell unearthed the stone cross, composed of fifteen stones in one direction and thirteen in the other, perhaps a reference to the year of Juan Ponce's landing, 1513. Nearby McConnell also discovered a small silver urn with a piece of parchment inside; the words on the parchment, in Spanish, seemed to confirm the authenticity of the site as that of Ponce's discovery, according to the booklet.

In his 1985 book *Up for Grabs*, John Rothchild wrote that the parchment is kept in a safe-deposit box. When the *Saturday Evening Post* challenged the site's authenticity in the 1940s, the owners of the attraction sued the magazine for libel and won, according to Rothchild.

Here's an interesting side note: Before her arrival in Florida in 1904, Dr. McConnell—aka "Diamond Lil"— gained international renown as one of the few female "stampeders" of the Klondike gold rush of the 1890s. She's credited with being the founder of St. Augustine's Fountain of Youth tourist attraction in 1904.

Although historians say the attraction's connection to Ponce is questionable, it has endured in the age of corporate theme parks. Visitors can still sip water from the Fountain near the coquina cross, see re-creations of a Timucuan village, enjoy an educational journey across the Atlantic in a planetarium, and tour grounds filled with colorful peacocks. On the way out, they can visit a well-stocked gift shop that offers for sale samples of the famed water in every size from a small vial to a large bottle.

After Visiting the Fountain of Youth,
This is How I Feel
St. Augustine, Florida

209

FOUNTAIN OF YOUTH

WALT

DISCOVER THE HISTORIC
Fountain of Youth
ST. AUGUSTINE, FLA.

Ponce de Leon's
Fountain of Youth
Authentic
Spring Water
St. Augustine, Florida

LARGE
BOTTLES
3.50

Authentic
Spring Water
St. Augustine, Florida

Statue of Juan Ponce de Leon in Fountain of Youth Park. St. Augustine, Florida

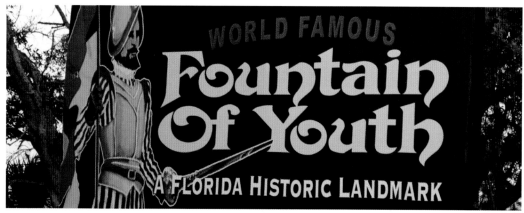

WORLD FAMOUS
Fountain
Of Youth
A FLORIDA HISTORIC LANDMARK

St. Petersburg, Florida. To the Fountain of Youth.

Bayfront to Baseball Park: St. Petersburg's Fountain

Although the Fountain of Youth attraction in St. Augustine is the best-known Florida site with an advertised link to Ponce's magic waters, it's certainly not alone. St. Petersburg, on the opposite coast of Florida from Ponce's initial landing, once had a well-known "fountain of youth." It began with wealthy philanthropist Edwin H. Tomlinson, who built a long fishing pier there at the beginning of the twentieth century.

At the end of the pier, which stretched out into Tampa Bay, Tomlinson built a fishing cottage with a well that was said to have a strong taste of sulfur. In 1908, Dr. Jesse Conrad bought the property and opened a spa where customers could bathe in the well's water and even drink it. It was Conrad who named the well the "Fountain of Youth."

In 1911, the City of St. Petersburg purchased the location, and after the pier was destroyed in a 1921 hurricane, the city built a fountain on land to provide access to the water, which was found to contain high amounts of lithium.

The fountain "attracted tourists and residents for more than six decades, . . . despite its pungent odor," writes St. Petersburg historian Scott Taylor Hartzell. "Many persons here drink that water exclusively and attribute to it great virtues,"

S. 43—Fountain of Youth
St. Petersburg, Fla. "The Sunshine City"

Fountain of Youth
ST. PETERSBURG, FLA., "The Sunshine City"

a 1938 article in the city's *Evening Independent* newspaper noted.

Ironically, the original well from the Fountain of Youth pier still bubbles up in the bay. About a block away from the original land-based fountain, St. Petersburg's Fountain of Youth Park occupies a shady spot near Al Lang Baseball Stadium in the city's downtown. A drinking fountain takes center stage, flanked by two wall-mounted water fountains in the shape of lions' heads and fronted by a sign emblazoned with "Fountain of Youth" in medieval-looking script.

Above and facing page: St. Petersburg's Fountain of Youth through the years from a well on a pier to a small park near Al Lang Stadium.

SARASOTA
COUNTY
LAND OF THE
real FOUNTAIN OF YOUTH

SARASOTA
COUNTY
LAND OF THE
real FOUNTAIN OF YOUTH

WARM
Mineral Springs

12 MILES SOUTH OF VENICE, FLORIDA

WARM
Mineral Springs

12 MILES SOUTH OF VENICE, FLORIDA

Florida's Famed Health Spa
WARM MINERAL SPRINGS
"THE REAL FOUNTAIN OF YOUTH"
VENICE, FLORIDA

A mid-twentieth-century brochure (*left*) and postcard (*above*) promoting Warm Springs and Sarasota County.

Facing page, top: Vintage photo of visitors at the spring. *Bottom*: Today the spring is co-owned by the county and the City of North Port and continues to attract visitors seeking its healing effects.

Spa with Saber-Tooths: Warm Mineral Springs

About seventy miles south of St. Petersburg, not far from Venice in Sarasota County, lies another "fountain of youth" that's rich in history: Warm Mineral Springs, thought to be Florida's only "hot" springs. High in mineral content, the water is also anaerobic—lacking in oxygen—which has helped preserve incredible archaeological finds, including the bones of saber-tooth tigers and an 11,000-year-old man. The archaeological value of the site led to a listing on the National Register of Historic Places in 1977.

A spa opened at the springs in the 1950s, and the site still offers a health spa, advertised in 2012 as "America's Natural Wellness Destination." Varied treatments are available, in addition to dips in the 87-degree water, which is advertised as providing relief for muscular problems, arthritis, and rheumatism, as well as other benefits.

Today Warm Mineral Springs seems to be especially popular with European visitors to Florida. Outside the spring, in front of a spurting fountain, a plaque proclaims that, "according to authentic historical documents, this warm salt spring is the Fountain of Youth sought vainly by Ponce de León."

PONCE DE LEON SPRINGS

THE FOUNTAIN OF YOUTH

MAKE A DATE WITH HISTORY!
Ponce de Leon Springs
NATURE'S "CAMERALAND"

Central Florida Favorite: Ponce de Leon Springs

In Volusia County, about thirty miles from Florida's east coast and forty-five miles from Orlando, visitors can find the Florida spring that's linked to Ponce de León in name as well as myth. In 2011, a website dubbed the De Leon Springs Inquisitioner summarized the history of the spring this way: "For ten thousand years people hunted, fished, and farmed the area. Then one day some Europeans, who were lost, showed up and declared that they discovered the springs and owned it. Things went down hill from there."

As with most of Florida's major springs, evidence indicates that humans have visited or lived at De Leon Springs for thousands of years. "Native Americans occupied the area periodically from as early as 8000 BC," according to a state website. "A 6,000-year-old dugout canoe, one of the oldest ever found in America, was discovered here."

During the colonial and territorial periods, settlers built farms in the area that eventually became sugar and cotton plantations. In 1823, a Revolutionary War veteran from South Carolina, Maj. Joseph Woodruff, began the first plantation on the site and named it Spring Garden. In 1831, Woodruff's land became the property of another South Carolina planter, Col. Orlando Rees, who in 1832 hosted naturalist John James Audubon

THE HOTEL PONCE DE LEON SPRINGS "THE FOUNTAIN OF YOUTH"
DE LEON SPRINGS, FLORIDA
D-426

Above: A vintage postcard shows the Ponce de León Springs Inn, built in the 1920s. *Facing page, top*: A graphic from a De Leon Springs brochure features an infant Juan Ponce in a diaper. *Bottom*: A painted sign shows Juan Ponce with a bathing beauty in homage to the statue that used to be posed near the park's entrance.